SELF-CARE
101

---

30 Days to 101 Ways of Self-Care
A Journal of Discovery

For Taylor –

Enjoy the journey!

Tend what you like + love.

Love –
Lee Ann

Dolphin Publishing Company
Florida

Text ©2019 LeeAnn Kendall
Cover ©2019 Dolphin Publishing Company
LeeAnnKendall.com

ISBN: 9781689184298

Distributed in the US by Dolphin Publishing Company
St. Augustine, FL 32086

To my mother, Joan,

and my husband, Steve:

You make this life beautiful.

Thank you for your loving support and encouragement.

I love you.

xoxo

SELF-CARE 101

30 Days to 101 Ways of Self-Care
A Journal of Discovery

BY LEEANN S. KENDALL

**DOLPHIN PUBLISHING
COMPANY**

This journal belongs to

_____

A NOTE FROM THE AUTHOR

Take a few minutes every day, and at the end
of 30 days, you'll have 101 ways of self-care.
Discover what makes you feel good and well,
and find long forgotten and new creative
ways that make you happy.

Enjoy the process, and have fun.

Happy Discovery!

now ideas self wanted
spirit friends outdoors health
inner loyalty mind family
peace purity strength innocence nature prosperity appreciate compassion balance grown always great
body financial
famous dreams connected flexibility love projects little
feel kindness vitality self-forgiveness boundaries
elegance integrity acceptance attitude creative
energy freedom kinder joy power express

How this Journal Works

So often we put our attention outside ourselves
for happiness. Whether we are focused on things, relationships,
or accomplishments, we often come up wanting.
The truth is, happiness is an inside job.

This journal is a path back to yourself. Each day answer
one question in a variety of ways, journal about WHY it matters
to you, and feel the feelings of each of your choices.
When you finish each day, transfer the answers to the back of
the book. At the end of 30 days, you'll have 101 personal
ways that bring you happiness, love, and joy.

By tapping into your sources of joy, you are creating a
map of self-care. You're creating a template that you can turn to
time and time again to tap into your natural joy.

It seems so simple, and it is. Don't let the simplicity
fool you. Sometimes it is the little things that can be the
most profound. Take the time to connect with yourself and
uncover what has the power to move you.

I wish you a powerful and joyful journey of self-discovery.

Be in touch @leeannkendall #selfcare101 #selfcare
www.leeannkendall.com

INTRODUCTION

Reinventing my life at age 31, I needed help. Luckily, I found a good therapist who would help me get back on track. One of the most critical transitions happened when she asked me this simple question:

"So, what do you like to do?

When you're not working and not sleeping, what do you like to do?"

"Huh?" I didn't have an answer.

After three years of intense physical and emotional labor of running restaurants and publishing a restaurant guide, I was working day and night. When I wasn't working, I was numbing myself with alcohol.

I'd recently discovered yoga, and found it was an excellent way for me to relax and get away from my crazy life. But in terms of what else I liked to do, or what brought me joy, I was completely blank. The truth is, I had abandoned myself and gotten lost in someone else's dreams. I didn't have my own answers.

Armed with this simple question, and an assignment to find out what I like, what I love and enjoy, I set out on an adventure of self-discovery. This journal is the response to that journey. In the process, I discovered self-care as a way to reconnect with myself and long-lost dreams and desires.

Over the years, self-care has been an evolving model for staying connected with my heart and being true to myself. When I get off track, I always have a way home, a map of sorts. When I lose energy and get exhausted, I know it's because I have not been taking good enough care of myself. Returning to this list, time and time again, I find my way back home. I revisit it and can update the questions and answers to fit my current life.

I'm sharing this journal as a fun and straightforward path of self-discovery. If this helps you feel more connected and in touch with your inner power and joy, then this journal is successful.

Take a few minutes each day to answer these simple questions to build your self-care map.

It is simple and it's profound. Each day answer one question with three to four different answers. Then transfer those answers to the back of the book, to your Self-Care Map.

Before you get started, realize that contrary to popular belief, self-care is not selfish. Self-care is the way to be responsible for your happiness and help others to do the same. When you're filled up and content, you have a lot more to give. When someone asks you what you like to do, or wants to share meaningful time, you'll have your go-to list. When you know yourself better, you can help others understand you better, and vice versa. Share this book and concept with everyone you know, and soon we'll have more self-loving, self-responsible people all over the planet. Enjoy the journey. Let's get started.

"Self-care
is how you take
your power back."

~ Lalah Delia

DAY
1

Today I can feel joy when I...

1. _____
2. _____
3. _____

What about these experiences bring me joy?
Why do these make happy?

Be specific. Get as detailed as possible. Feel it.

_____
_____
_____
_____
_____
_____
_____
_____
_____
_____
_____
_____

_____

_____

_____

_____

_____

_____

_____

_____

_____

_____

_____

_____

_____

_____

_____

_____

_____

_____

_____

_____

"Sometimes your joy is the source of your smile,
but sometimes your smile can be the source of your joy."

~ Thich Nhat Hanh

DAY 2

I feel connected when I

4. _____
5. _____
6. _____

Why? What about these experiences helps me feel connected? What feels so good?

Be specific. Get as detailed as possible. Feel it.

_____

_____

_____

_____

_____

_____

_____

_____

_____

_____

_____

_____

_____

DAY
3

When I was little, I loved to

7. _____
8. _____
9. _____

Why? What about these experiences did I love?

Be specific. Get as detailed as possible. Feel it.

_____
_____
_____
_____
_____
_____
_____
_____
_____
_____
_____

DAY
4

I always thought,
"When I grow up, I will _____."
Today I can _____.

10. _____

11. _____

12. _____

Why did I want to do this when I was young?
Why do I want to do this now?
What can I put in my schedule this week? Do it.

Be specific. Get as detailed as possible. Feel it.

_____

_____

_____

_____

_____

_____

_____

_____

_____

_____

"Start where you are. Use what you have. Do what you can."

~ Arthur Ashe

DAY 5

What can I do for my state-of-mind right now, that will be helpful and feel good?

13. _____

14. _____

15. _____

Why did I pick this? What about this feels good?

Be specific. Get as detailed as possible. Feel it.

_____

_____

_____

_____

_____

_____

_____

_____

_____

_____

_____

_____

"You, yourself, as much as anybody else in the entire universe, deserve your love and affection."

~Buddha

DAY
6

What childhood dreams do I still want to fulfill?

16. _____

17. _____

18. _____

Why do I still want these dreams to come true?
What part of me is holding back from going for it?
How can I let go of the resistance?
What will it feel like when I do this?

Be specific. Get as detailed as possible. Feel it.

_____

_____

_____

_____

_____

_____

_____

_____

_____

_____

_____

_____

_____

_____

_____

_____

_____

_____

_____

_____

_____

_____

_____

_____

_____

_____

_____

_____

_____

_____

"If you can dream it, you can do it."
~Walt Disney

DAY
7

Something I have always wanted to do, but have avoided.

19. _____

20. _____

21. _____

Why do I still want to do it? What do I think it will feel like? Why does this make me excited and happy? What was stopping me?

Be specific. Get as detailed as possible. Feel it.

_____

_____

_____

_____

_____

_____

_____

_____

_____

_____

_____

_____

_____

_____

_____

_____

_____

_____

_____

_____

_____

_____

_____

_____

_____

_____

_____

_____

_____

_____

_____

_____

_____

_____

_____

"Fear regret more than failure."

~Taryn Rose

DAY
8

If I were famous, I would

22. _____
23. _____
24. _____

**Why would I want to do that? How would I feel?
Do I need to wait until I am famous, or can I do it now?**

Be specific. Get as detailed as possible. Feel it.

_____
_____
_____
_____
_____
_____
_____
_____
_____
_____
_____
_____

_____

_____

_____

_____

_____

_____

_____

_____

_____

_____

_____

_____

_____

_____

_____

_____

_____

_____

_____

_____

_____

"People confuse fame with validation or love.

But fame is not the reward.
The reward is getting fulfillment out of doing the thing you love."

~Claire Danes

DAY 9

What can I do outdoors today?

25. _____
26. _____
27. _____

Why? How will I feel?
Imagine it clearly. Fill in the details.

Be specific. Get as detailed as possible. Feel it.

_____

_____

_____

_____

_____

_____

_____

_____

_____

_____

_____

_____

_____

_____

_____

_____

_____

_____

_____

_____

_____

_____

_____

_____

_____

_____

_____

_____

_____

_____

_____

_____

_____

"A ship in a harbor is safe, but it's not what ships are built for."

~ John A. Shedd

DAY
10

What attitude can I update?
What's a good replacement?

28. _____
29. _____
30. _____

Why? How will I feel? Imagine it clearly.
Fill in the details. What does it cost me to hang on to this
old way of being? What's possible if I transform it?

Be specific. Get as detailed as possible. Feel it.

_____
_____
_____
_____
_____
_____
_____
_____
_____
_____
_____
_____

_____

_____

_____

_____

_____

_____

_____

_____

_____

_____

_____

_____

_____

_____

_____

_____

_____

_____

"The greatest discovery of all time is that a person can change his future by merely changing his attitude."

~Oprah Winfrey

DAY
11

Just for today, I will do something for a family member or friend.

31. _____

32. _____

33. _____

Why do I want to do that? How will I feel?

Be specific. Get as detailed as possible. Feel it.

_____

_____

_____

_____

_____

_____

_____

_____

_____

_____

_____

_____

_____

_____

_____

_____

_____

_____

_____

_____

_____

_____

_____

_____

_____

_____

_____

_____

_____

_____

_____

_____

_____

_____

_____

_____

_____

"Love and kindness are never wasted. They always make a difference.
They bless the one who receives them, and they bless you, the giver."

~Barbara De Angelis

DAY 12

What part of my life could benefit from greater self-acceptance?

34. _____

35. _____

36. _____

Why do I want to do that? How does this feel? If I continue to do this, how will it impact my daily experience?

Be specific. Get as detailed as possible. Feel it.

_____

_____

_____

_____

_____

_____

_____

_____

_____

_____

_____

_____

_____

_____

_____

_____

_____

_____

_____

_____

_____

_____

_____

_____

_____

_____

_____

_____

_____

_____

_____

"Let go of who you think you are supposed to be and be who you are."

~Brené Brown

DAY
13

If I am kinder to myself, and stop judging myself, what new thoughts will I be thinking?

13. _____

14. _____

15. _____

How does that feel? How does changing thoughts change my life?

Be specific. Get as detailed as possible. Feel it.

_____

_____

_____

_____

_____

_____

_____

_____

_____

_____

_____

_____

_____

_____

_____

_____

_____

_____

_____

_____

_____

_____

_____

_____

_____

_____

_____

_____

_____

_____

_____

"To fall in love with yourself
is the first secret of happiness."
~ Robert Morley

"It's
not what you look
at that matters,
it's what you see."
~ Henry David Thoreau

F. L. Y.

First Love Yourself

DAY
14

What creative ideas or projects can I work on that will make me happy?

40. _____

41. _____

42. _____

How will that make me feel? What kind of inner resources do I need to bring to this?

Be specific. Get as detailed as possible. Feel it.

_____

_____

_____

_____

_____

_____

_____

_____

_____

_____

_____

_____

_____

_____

_____

_____

_____

_____

_____

_____

_____

_____

_____

_____

_____

_____

_____

_____

_____

_____

_____

_____

"There is a vitality, a life force, an energy, a quickening that is translated through you into action, and because there is only one of you in all of time, this expression is unique. And if you block it, it will never exist through any other medium and it will be lost."

~ Martha Graham

DAY
15

How can I express love today?
Who can I help?

43. _____

44. _____

45. _____

How does it feel just thinking about it?
How can I bring this feeling into my life every day?
Why does that matter?

Be specific. Get as detailed as possible. Feel it.

_____

_____

_____

_____

_____

_____

_____

_____

_____

_____

_____

_____

_____

_____

_____

_____

_____

_____

_____

_____

_____

_____

_____

_____

_____

_____

_____

_____

_____

_____

_____

_____

_____

_____

_____

"We are shaped and fashioned by what we love."
~ Goethe

DAY
16

What we appreciate, appreciates.
Finish this sentence.
I appreciate that I am

46. _____

47. _____

48. _____

Why does this feel so good?

Be specific. Get as detailed as possible. Feel it.

_____

_____

_____

_____

_____

_____

_____

_____

_____

_____

_____

_____

_____

_____

_____

_____

_____

_____

_____

_____

_____

_____

_____

_____

_____

_____

_____

_____

_____

_____

*"Simply give to yourselves that which you need – which is love
and appreciation without judgment."*

~ Réné Gaudette

DAY
17

What idea wants to come through me?

49. _____

50. _____

51. _____

Which idea do I want to develop?

Be specific. Get as detailed as possible. Feel it.

_____

_____

_____

_____

_____

_____

_____

_____

_____

_____

_____

_____

_____

_____

_____

_____

_____

_____

_____

_____

_____

_____

_____

_____

_____

_____

_____

_____

_____

_____

_____

_____

"A good idea becomes a great idea when you let it out."

~ Unknown

DAY 18

What kind act do I do for others, that I can do for myself, today?

52. _____

53. _____

54. _____

How will that make me feel?
Why should I make sure I schedule this?

Be specific. Get as detailed as possible. Feel it.

_____

_____

_____

_____

_____

_____

_____

_____

_____

_____

_____

"Self-care is not selfish. You cannot serve from an empty vessel."

~ Eleanor Brownn

DAY
19

**What can I do in my finances that
will bring me more peace?**

55. _____

56. _____

57. _____

58. _____

**What does it feel like to see this as already
accomplished? What will it feel like when it's done?**

Be specific. Get as detailed as possible. Feel it.

_____

_____

_____

_____

_____

_____

_____

_____

_____

_____

_____

_____

_____

_____

_____

_____

_____

_____

_____

_____

_____

_____

_____

_____

_____

_____

_____

_____

_____

_____

_____

"The secret to getting ahead is getting started. The secret to getting started is breaking your complex overwhelming tasks into small manageable tasks and then starting on the first one."

~ Mark Twain

DAY 20

What activity can I do that will bring more energy and vitality into my body? How can I make it fun?

59. _____

60. _____

61. _____

62. _____

How will that make me feel? How does that inspire me?

Be specific. Get as detailed as possible. Feel it.

_____

_____

_____

_____

_____

_____

_____

_____

_____

_____

_____

_____

_____

_____

_____

_____

_____

_____

_____

_____

_____

_____

_____

_____

_____

_____

_____

_____

_____

_____

"The higher your energy level, the more efficient your body.
The more efficient your body, the better you feel, and the more you
will use your talent to produce outstanding results."

~ Tony Robbins

DAY
21

What can I do for my body that is loving and kind?

63._____

64._____

65._____

Just imagining it, I feel better. Why does self-care for my body feel so good? How can I make sure that I am giving this to myself all the time?

Be specific. Get as detailed as possible. Feel it.

_____

_____

_____

_____

_____

_____

_____

_____

_____

_____

_____

_____

_____

_____

_____

_____

_____

_____

_____

_____

_____

_____

_____

_____

_____

_____

_____

_____

_____

_____

_____

_____

_____

"To love oneself is the beginning of a lifelong romance."

~ Oscar Wilde

DAY
22

What can I do to show my body acceptance and compassion?

66. _____

67. _____

68. _____

69. _____

What do I want to say? How do I feel when I am so compassionate to myself?

Be specific. Get as detailed as possible. Feel it.

_____

_____

_____

_____

_____

_____

_____

_____

_____

_____

_____

_____

_____

_____

_____

_____

_____

_____

_____

_____

_____

_____

_____

_____

_____

_____

_____

_____

_____

_____

_____

_____

"'You have peace,' the old woman said,
'when you make it with yourself.'"

~Mitch Albom

DAY
23

What decision or choice did I make earlier in my life, that I wish I did differently? What action can I take now?

70.
71.
72.
73.

What if I forgave myself right here and right now? What if I let myself off the hook and accept everything is working out for the highest good of all concerned? How does that feel? Woohoo!

Be specific. Get as detailed as possible. Feel it.

_____

_____

_____

_____

_____

_____

_____

_____

_____

_____

_____

_____

_____

_____

_____

_____

_____

_____

_____

_____

_____

"Forgiving yourself, believing in yourself, and choosing to love yourself are the best gifts one could receive."

~ Brittany Burgunder

DAY
24

What step can I take towards being healthier?

74. _____

75. _____

76. _____

77. _____

What difference will it make?
How will it make me feel if I do this?

Be specific. Get as detailed as possible. Feel it.

_____

_____

_____

_____

_____

_____

_____

_____

_____

_____

_____

_____

_____

_____

_____

_____

_____

_____

_____

_____

_____

_____

_____

_____

_____

_____

_____

_____

_____

_____

_____

_____

_____

"The first wealth is health."
~ Ralph Waldo Emerson

DAY
25

What step can I take towards having more freedom?

78._____

79._____

80._____

81._____

What will greater freedom give me? How will I feel?

Be specific. Get as detailed as possible. Feel it.

_____

_____

_____

_____

_____

_____

_____

_____

_____

_____

_____

_____

"*The most courageous act is still to think for yourself. Aloud.*"

~ Coco Chanel

DAY
26

What can I do to experience more joy?

82. _____

83. _____

84. _____

85. _____

If I am experiencing more joy, what else is possible?
Why do I want to be more joyful? What else is possible?

Be specific. Get as detailed as possible. Feel it.

_____

_____

_____

_____

_____

_____

_____

_____

_____

_____

_____

_____

_____

_____

_____

_____

_____

_____

_____

_____

_____

_____

_____

_____

_____

_____

_____

_____

_____

_____

"There are two ways of spreading light: to be the candle or the mirror that reflects it."

~ Edith Wharton

DAY
27

_____

How can I love myself even more today?

86. _____

87. _____

88. _____

89. _____

**What will that feel like? How much better will
it make me feel if I am loving myself? Who else
and what else will it impact?**

Be specific. Get as detailed as possible. Feel it.

_____

_____

_____

_____

_____

_____

_____

_____

_____

_____

_____

_____

_____

_____

_____

_____

_____

_____

_____

_____

_____

_____

_____

_____

_____

_____

_____

_____

_____

_____

_____

"Love yourself first, because that's who you'll be spending the rest of your life with."

~ Unknown

DAY
28

What can I let go of in order to be happier right now?

90. _____

91. _____

92. _____

93. _____

What does is feel like when I let go? How can I let go faster? What will that do for my overall happiness?

Be specific. Get as detailed as possible. Feel it.

_____

_____

_____

_____

_____

_____

_____

_____

_____

_____

_____

_____

_____

_____

_____

_____

_____

_____

_____

_____

_____

_____

_____

_____

_____

_____

_____

_____

_____

_____

_____

_____

_____

"When I let go of what I am, I become what I might be.
When I let go of what I have, I receive what I need."

~ Tao Te Ching

DAY
29

How can I create a powerful vision for my life?

94. _____

95. _____

96. _____

97. _____

Why would I want to do that? Once I do, what will that help me do? How will I feel? What's my vision?

Be specific. Get as detailed as possible. Feel it.

_____

_____

_____

_____

_____

_____

_____

_____

_____

_____

_____

_____

_____

_____

_____

_____

_____

_____

_____

_____

_____

_____

_____

_____

_____

_____

_____

_____

_____

_____

_____

_____

"Vision is the art of seeing things invisible."
~ Jonathan Swift

DAY
30

**What do I want to do in this life that
I have been holding back on?**

98._____

99._____

100._____

101. _____

**What's holding me back? How can I take action anyway?
How will I feel while I'm doing this?
How will completing this make me feel?**

Be specific. Get as detailed as possible. Feel it.

_____

_____

_____

_____

_____

_____

_____

_____

_____

_____

_____

_____

_____

_____

_____

_____

_____

_____

_____

_____

_____

_____

_____

_____

_____

_____

_____

_____

_____

_____

_____

_____

_____

"Tell me, what is it you plan to do with your one wild and precious life?"

~ Mary Oliver

"At the end of our life our questions are simple: Did I live fully? Did I love well?"

~ Jack Kornfield

My Self-Care Map

1.

2.

3.

4.

5.

6.

7.

8.

9.

10.

11.

12.

13.

14.

15.

16.

17.

18.

19.

20.

21.

22.

23.

24.

25.

26.

27.

28.

29.

30.

31.

32.

33.

34.

35.

36.

37.

38.

39.

40.

41.

42.

43.

44.

45.

46.

47.

48.

49.

50.

51.

52.

53.

54.

55.

56.

57.

58.

59.

60.

61.

62.

63.

64.

65.

66.

67.

68.

69.

70.

71.

72.

73.

74.

75.

76.

77.

78.

79.

80.

81.

82.

83.

84.

85.

86.

87.

88.

89.

90.

91.

92.

93.

94.

95.

96.

97.

98.

99.

100.

101.

ABOUT THE AUTHOR

LeeAnn Kendall loves books and nature, spirituality
and transformation. At age four, she started copying
sacred texts long hand and wanted to know God. Being
a published author has been her lifelong dream.
She considers life a spiritual journey and is
grateful to be alive at this exciting time.

Self-care first came to LeeAnn while attending the
University of Santa Monica, a school whose curriculum
guides students to know themselves as their loving
essence. This journal is the result of her thesis and is
intended to help you connect to your loving essence.

LeeAnn is a devoted daughter, sister, wife,
friend, teacher and cat lover.

She lives in St. Augustine, Florida,
with her husband, Steve.